Abracadbra
to
Zany

A
Smorgasbord
of
Birthday Party Vendors
in
Central & Eastern
Massachusetts

Birthday Wishes and Smiling Kids

I'd like to introduce you to these two amazing organizations if you haven't already heard about them. Partnered together, Birthday Wishes provides children living in shelters with birthday parties while Smiling Kids helps with the birthday presents. Helping bring joy to over 900 children each year, the programs are a wonderful way to give back to the community.
For more information on either organization please visit their websites
www.smilingkidsinc.org and
www.birthdaywishes.org

.

Thank You

Lisa Welsh for all her help with publicity
Kara Andrews for answering all my marketing related questions
John Smith for all his help with the 2009 fundraiser expo
Lisa Vasiloff & Karen Sommers and the rest of the crew at Birthday Wishes and Smiling Kids for bringing smiles to children in shelters
Linda Griffin for taking all the pictures
Crystal Waterman for her opinion on the cover.
Robert Griffin for his help with the editing.

All the women who pointed me to various mom and entrepreneur related websites
And of course all the moms in Massachusetts who gave my book a chance

Dedication

To Sunny, Joe, Peter T. and Pete
For putting up with a cranky mommy and wife,
who saw the sunrise a few
too many times while trying to get in extra book
time.

Introduction

So many things come about by people trying to fill a niche, by thinking to themselves "Geez, I wish I had something that _____". When they can't find the something that fills in that blank, whatever it may be, they make it themselves. And that is how "Abracadbra to Zany" was born.

Last spring I was perusing the local parenting papers and came across the birthday party advertisements in each. I knew there had to be more out there than what was listed so I went looking for a centralized database or book but came up empty-handed. Some websites were more inclusive than others but nothing had what I was looking for.

I decided it was time to fill in that blank and write it myself. Every region of Central and Eastern Massachusetts and every category I could think of is covered. So if you're looking for a clown that services Worcester County or a roller skating rink on the South Shore, it's here. Every vendor provided their permission to be listed.

In some cases I have included vendors who provide a unique service and cater to the coverage area or have multiple locations, some of which fall outside the area. I plan on revising the book in the Fall of 2009 for additional vendors who would like to be listed. They can contact me at birthdaydirectory@gmail.com . I hope you enjoy the book as much as I did researching and writing it. *And always: protect yourself and your family by checking out the reviews, credentials and references of a vendor before you hire them.*

Table of Contents

Product Vendors

Bakeries & Cakes

Babycakes
Location: Boxborough, MA 01719
Ph: 508-212-2789
Web: www.babycakesandconfections.com
Email: babycakesandconfections@comcast.net

Baker's Dozen
Location: Cape Cod
Ph: 508-367-2058
Web: www.bakeme13.com
Email: info@bakeme13.com

Cake by Paula Surrette
Location: Bridgewater MA 02324
Ph: 508-415-9890
    508-697-1147
Web: www.cakebypaulasurrette.com
Email: cakebypaula@yahoo.com

Dessertworks
Location: 38 Vanderbilt Ave
    Norwood, MA 02062
Ph: 781-769-1133
Fax: 781-769-3133
Web: www.dessertworks.net
Email: staff@dessertworks.net

Goldie the Clown
See also Entertainment Providers: Clowns
Location: Rockland, MA 02370
Ph: 781-771-7828
Web: http://alwayzzzeatcake.blogspot.com
Email: goldietheclown@aol.com

Montilio's Bakery

Web: www.montilios.com
Email: george@montilios.com
Locations: 134 Spark St.
              Brockton, MA 02302
              Ph: 508-894-8855

              619 Main St.
              Centreville MA 02632
              Ph: 508-894-8855

              638 Adams St.
              Quincy, MA 02169
              Ph: 617-472-5500

Panorama Bakery

Mailing Address:
              PO Box 111
              Waban, MA 02468
Ph: 617-332-4445(office)
              617-332-4242(bakery)
Fax: 617-965-8167
Web: www.panoramabakery.com
Email: sofia@bigskybreads.com
Locations: 105 Union St.
              Newton Centre, MA 02459

              351 Newton St.
              Waltham, MA 02468

Balloons

Balloons All Over

Location:	164 Milk St.
	Westboro, MA 01581
Ph:	508-366-6307
Web:	www.balloonsallover.com
Email:	balloonsallover@aol.com

Wow! Effect, Inc.

Location:	Cambridge, MA
Ph:	617-201-2525
Web:	www.wowballoons.com
Email:	contact@wowballoons.com

Costumes

Boston Costume

Location: 200 Broadway
        Cambridge, MA 02139
Ph: 888-482-1632
Web: www.bostoncostume.com
Email: service@bostoncostume.com

Joker's Wild

Web: www.thejokerswild.com
Email: wildjoke@aol.com
Locations: 87 Andover St.
         Danvers, MA 01923
         Ph: 978-777-7206

         204 N. Main St.
         North Reading, MA 01864
         Ph: 978-664-5401

Favors

A Sweet Reward
Location: Boxford, MA 01921
Ph: 978-590-3335
               978-561-1705
Fax: 978-359-0229
Web: www.asweetreward.com
Email: info@asweetreward.com

4 Sisters Soaps
Location: Malden, MA 02148
Ph: 781-322-6888
Web: www.4sisterssoaps.com
Email: mama@4sisterssoaps.com

Massachusetts Bay Trading Company
Location: 120 Concord Rd
               Weston, MA 02493
Ph: 508-415-1966
Fax: 781-998-0593
Web: www.massbaytrading.com
Email: questions@massbaytrading.com

Priscilla's Candies
Web: www.priscillacandies.com
Email: Rhonda@priscillacandies.com
Locations: 428 Essex St.
               Lawrence, MA 01840
               Ph: 978-682-2893

               25 Crystal Ave
               Derry, NH 03038
               Ph: 603-432-3838

Invitations & Stationary

Dundee Printing
Location: 30 Dundee Dr.
                Bridgewater, MA 02324
Ph: 508-279-3327
Web: www.dundeeprinting.com
Email: sales@dundeeprinting.com

Invitations & Company
Location: 9 Hawthorne Place
                Boston, MA 02114
Ph: 617-227-2127
Fax: 617-227-8515
Web: www.bestinvite.com
Email: sales@bestinvite.com

Lady Slipper Stationary
Location: South Yarmouth MA
Ph: 877-394-6161(Toll Free)
                508-394-6161
Web: www.ladyslipperstationary.com
Email: Cyndi@ladyslipperstationary.com

The Invitation Source
Location: Mansfield, MA 02048
Ph: 508-337-4988
                877-341-1788 (Toll Free in MA)
Web: www.theinvitationsource.com
Email: invitationsource@aol.com
Contact: Sherri Blau

Posh Peacock

Mailing Address:

        PO Box 1427

        Arlington, MA 02474

Web: www.poshpeacock.com

Email: info@poshpeacock.com

Unique Simchas Invitations & Calligraphy

Location: 630 Commonwealth Ave

        Newton, MA 02459

Ph: 617-969-0118

Web: www.uniquesimchas.com

Email: uniqsimcha@aol.com

We Print Today

Location: 66 Summer Street

        Kingston MA 02364

Ph: 781-585-6021 x30

Fax: 781-582-1538

Web: www.weprinttoday.com

        www.createastamp.com

Email: info@weprinttoday.com

The Write Expression

Location: 46 Main St.

        Topsfield, MA 01983

Ph: 978-887-0330

Web: www.thewrite-expression.com

Email: info@thewrite-expression.com

Rental Companies

Backyard Movie Night
Location: Middleboro MA 02346
Ph: 508-813-6034
Web: www.backyardmovienite.com
Email: bookings@backyardmovienite.com
Contact: Cathy

Bay State Tent
Location: 150 Lorum St
                 Tewksbury, MA 01876
Ph: 800-439-5261
Web: www.baystatetent.com
Email: david@baystatetent.com
Contact: David Knight

Bouncin' For Fun LLC
Location: Mansfield, MA 02048
Ph: 508-718-5588
Web: www.bouncinforfun.com
Email: bouncinforfun@hotmail.com

Franklin Party Rentals
Location: 158 Grove St.
                 Franklin, MA 02038
Ph: 508-520-6566
Web: www.franklinpartyrentals.com
Email: info@franklinpartyrentals.com

Funzalo Foam Parties & Backyard Movies
Location: 25 Charles St.
                 Douglas, MA 01516
Ph: 508-735-9523
Web: www.funzaloparties.com
Email: funzaloparties@mca.com

Grant's Rental

Location: 10 Bedford Park
                  Bridgewater, MA 02324
Ph: 508-279-0950
Web: www.grantsrental.com
Email: bgrant@tmlp.com

Perfect Party Rentals

Web: www.perfectpartyrentals.net
Email: dmasison31@comcast.net
Locations: 31 Southpark Lane
                  Mansfield, MA 02048
                  Ph: 508-954-3014

                  252 Sandwich Rd.
                  Wareham, MA 02571
                  Ph: 508-295-8444

Taylor Rental of Sudbury

Location: 712 Boston Post Rd.
                  Sudbury, MA 01776
Ph: 978-443-7368
                  800-564-7368
                  (Toll Free Eastern MA only)
Web: www.sudburytaylor.com
Email: rent@sudburytaylor.com

Total Entertainment

See Entertainment Vendors: Ent. Provider Groups
Location: 123 Liberty St.
                  Danvers, MA 01923
Ph: 978-777-2050
Web: www.totalentertainment.biz
Email: total1@aol.com

Videographers & Slideshow
Production Companies

RUINNY Slideshow Production

Location:	Cambridge, MA
Ph:	617-460-4768
Web:	http://ruinny.com/
Email:	info@ruinny.com

Watch Me Grow Productions

See also Entertainment Vendors: Unique

Location:	Holden, MA 01520
Ph:	508-852-3749
Web:	www.watchmegrowproductions.com
Email:	amy@watchmegrowproductions.com

Entertainment Vendors

Please note that each individual vendor has their own preferred travel areas. Some travel state-wide and beyond while others will only attend events local to their area. It is best to check with each as to their policies regarding locations.

Airbrush Artists

Gin C. Productions
Location: Revere, MA 02151
Ph: 617-610-4720(cell)
                 781-286-5513(office)
Web: www.gincproductions.com
Email: gincproductions@aol.com

Kelly's Temporary Tattoos
Location: Cape Cod/Mashpee, MA
Ph: 239-821-3844
Web: www.kellytats.com
Email: Kelly@kellytats.com

Animals & Ponies

Animal Adventures
Location: 336 Sugar Rd
Bolton MA 01740
Ph: 978-779-8988
Web: www.animaladventures.net
Email: info@animaladventures.net
Contact: Brianna, Ed & Staff

Animal Affair
Location: 418 Fairview Ave
Rehoboth, MA 02769
Ph: 508-252-4252
Web: www.animalaffair.net

Animal Hour
Location: West Wareham, MA 02576
Ph: 508-273-7484
Web: www.animalhourparties.com
Email: info@animalhour.com

Animal World Experience
Location: Stoughton, MA
Mailing Address:
PO Box 754
Stoughton, MA 02072
Ph: 781-436-5400 (office)
781-974-6361 (cell)
Web: www.animalworldexperience.com
Email: info@animalworldexperience.com

Bugworks LLC
Location: 25 Wadsworth Road
                Sudbury MA 01776
Ph: 508-561-0149
Web: www.bugworks.net
Email: bugworks@comcast.net
Contact: Andrea Kozol & Maire Anne Diamond

Creature Teachers
Location: Littleton, MA 01460
Ph: 978-952--0020
Web: www.thecreatureteachers.com
Email: thecreatureteachers@hotmail.com

Giddy Up Pony Rides at HyRidge Farms
Location: 705 Alger Street
                Winchendon MA 01475
Ph: 978-297-7421
Web: www.giddyupponyrides.com
Contact: Beth Daly

Jungle Encounters
Location: Uxbridge, MA 01569
Mailing Address:
                PO Box 108
                Uxbridge, MA 01569
Ph: 508-380-4722
Web: www.jungleencounters.org
Email: Debi@jungleencounters.org

Paul's Pony Parties
Location: Canton, Ma 02021
Ph: 781-828-7028
Web: http://members.aol.com/pony4party
Email: pony4party@aol.com

Paul's Reptile Circus

Location: 36 Woodside Ave
Winthrop, MA 02152
Ph: 617-846-2194
Web: www.paulsreptilecircus.net
Email: reptiles02148@aol.com

Ponytails Pony Parties

Location: Plympton, MA 02367
Ph: 781-585-5544
508-280-9413 (cell)
Web: www.ponytailsponyparties.com
Email: ponytailsponyparties@yahoo.com

(The) Well Dressed Pony

Location: Bedford, MA
Ph: 781-275-8154
Web: www.thewelldressedpony.com
Email: welldressedpony@yahoo.com

Art & Animal Stuffing

Let's Gogh Art

Location:	PO Box 664
	Lunenburg, MA 01462
Ph:	877-278-4644
	978-833-6067 (cell phone)
Web:	www.letsgoghart.com
Email:	art@letsgoghart.com
Contact:	Lynn Toomey

Noah's Ark Animal Workshop

See also
Beauty, Etiquette and Princess Parties: Bella Bee

Locations: Grafton, MA 01519
Ph: 508-865-1578
Web: www.Iluvnoah.com
Email: cvanroon@verizon.net

North Easton, MA 02356
Ph: 508-230-7978
Web: www.buttonwoodark.com
Email: naaw@comcast.net

Teddy Town to You

See also Clowns: Violet the Clown

Location:	Stoughton, MA 02072
Mailing Address:	
	PO Box 66
	Stoughton, MA 02072
Ph:	781-344-1852
Web:	www.teddytowntoyou.com
Email:	violettheclown@comcast.net

Beauty. Etiquette & Princess Parties

Affordable Princess Parties
Location: 11 Cypress Lane
                 Tyngsboro MA 01879
Ph: 978-649-3024
Web: www.affordableprincessparties.com
Email: Kathy@affordableprincessparties.com
Contact: Kathy Belanger

Bella Bee
See also.Art & Animal Stuffing: Noah's Ark
Locations: Grafton, MA 01519
             Ph: 508-865-1578
             Web: www.Iluvnoah.com
             Email: cvanroon@verizon.net

             North Easton, MA 02356
             Ph: 508-230-7978
             Web: www.buttonwoodark.com
             Email: naaw@comcast.net

Little Miss Princess Parties
Location: Hingham, MA
Ph: 781-749-6075
                 781-738-4351 (cell)
Web: www.missprincessparty.com
Email: kelleherlaura2000@yahoo.com

Princesses & Pollywogs
Location: 1 Field Terrace
                 Woburn, MA 01801
Ph: 617-538-8912
Web: www.princessesandpollywogs.com
Email: parties@princessesandpollywogs.com

Princess Sharon: Bring on the Sparkle!

Location:	Lynn, MA
Ph:	781-710-1118
Web:	www.princesssharon.com
Email:	Sharon@princesssharon.com

Royal Tea Parties by Lady J

Location:	Millis, MA 02054
Ph:	1-866-376-1110
Web:	www.royalteaparties.net
Email:	royalteaparties@juno.com

Caricature Artists

Caricatures by Michael Horvath
Location: Andover, MA 01810
Ph: 978-886-5366
Web: www.seemikedraw.com
Email: mike@seemikedraw.com

Neal Portnoy Art Studio
Ages 13 & up
Location: 22 Walnut St.
      Holden, MA 01520
Ph: 800-242-DRAW
      508-829-8000
Fax: 508-829-9137
Web: www.idrawpeople.com
Email: neal@idrawpeople.com

Partoons
Location: 7 Melvin Drive
      Oxford MA 01540
Ph: 508-987-9219
Web: www.partoons.net
Email: don@partoons.net
Contact: Don Landgren Jr

Clowns

A Cluster of Clowns & Santa
Location: 136 Bunker Hill Lane
                Quincy, MA 02169-6133
Ph: 617-471-0890
Web: www.sparklesandsanta.com
Email: clowneeee@aol.com

Cheesecake the Clown
Location: Wakefield MA 01880
Ph: 781-621-8434
Web: http://cheesecakeandfriends.com
Email: dana@cheesecakeandfriends.com
Contact: Dana Montgomery

Davey the Clown
Location: Jamaica Plain MA 02130
Ph: 617-524-9191
Web: www.daveytheclown.com
Email: daveytclown@comcast.net
Contact: David Holzman

Flippo the Clown
Location: West Boylston, MA 01583
Ph: 1-508-845-1458
                1-888-Flippo-5
Web: www.flippothejugglinclown.com
Email: flippotheclown@yahoo.com

Goldie the Clown
See also Product Vendors: Bakeries/Cakes
Location: Rockland, MA 02370
Ph: 781-771-7828
Web: http://alwayzzzeatcake.blogspot.com
Email: goldietheclown@aol.com

Jimbo Z Klown & Magic & Holiday Characters too
Location: Haverhill, MA
Ph: 978-321-6504
Web: www.jimbozklown.com

Petunia the Clown
Location: Reading MA 01867
Ph: 781-942-9902
Web: www.petuniatheclown.com
Email: petuniatheclown@gmail.com

Poppee & Co. Clowns
Location: East Bridgewater, MA 02333
Ph: 508-378-0142
Web: www.poppeecoclowns.com
Email: poppeecoclowns@gmail.com

Sodapop the Clown
Location: Westford, MA 01886
Ph: 978-392-1818
Web: www.sodapoptheclown.com
Email: sodapoptheclown@hotmail.com

Violet the Clown
See also Art & Animal Stuffing: Teddy Town to You
Location: Stoughton, MA 02072
Mailing Address:
      PO Box 66
      Stoughton, MA 02072
Ph: 781-344-1852
Web: www.violettheclown.com
Email: violettheclown@comcast.net

Disc Jockeys

A Touch of Class DJ's

Location: 318 Stearns Rd
Marlborough MA 01752
Ph: 508-229-0009
1-800-480-3200
508-395-4814 (emergency cell)
Web: www.atouchofclass.com
Email: atcodj@aol.com
Contact: Ken Cosco,
Chief Entertainment Officer

Curtis Knight

Location: Billerica, MA 01822
Mailing Address:
PO Box 5266
Billerica, MA 01822
Ph: 866-667-8910
978-667-8910
Web: www.curtisknight.com
Email: curtis@curtisknight.com

Music on the Move DJ Service

Location: Reading, MA 01867
Ph: 800-998-7153
Web: www.dj-entertainment.com
Email: musiconthemove@comcast.net
Contact: Justin Cheverie

R&R Productions

Location: 18 Washington St. #24
                     Canton, MA 02021
Ph: 888-250-6384
Fax: 508-857-3702
Web: www.rrpdjs.com
Email: rrpdjs@rrpdjs.com

Rogers Music Express

Location: 900 Hancock St.
                     Abington, MA 02351
Ph: 781-878-5551
                     339-788-1359 (cell)
Web: http://rogersmusicexpress.com
Email: rogersmusicexpress@yahoo.com

Steve Charette

See also Entertainment Vendors; Magicians
Location: Worcester, MA
Ph: 508-210-0340
                     508-926-9955
Web: www.magicsteve.com
Email: presto13@hotmail.com

Entertainment Provider Groups

Party Solutions Network
Location: Cambridge, MA
Ph: 888-206-4800
    617-354-5000
Web: www.clownsboston.com
Email: partysolutionsco@aol.com
Contact: Joseph Kirby

Total Entertainment
See also Product Vendors: Rental Companies
Location: 123 Liberty St.
    Danvers, MA 01923
Ph: 978-777-2050
Web: www.totalentertainment.biz
Email: total1@aol.com

Face Painters

Fabulous Facepainting
Location: East Bridgewater, MA 02333
Ph: 508-378-4396
Web: www.fabulousfacepainting.net
Email: annelkerrigan@comcast.net

Fictional Faces
Location: 39 Hudson St.
      Somerville, MA 02143
Ph: 617-625-0726
Web: www.fictionalfaces.com
Email: jmfall@comcast.net

Fun Faces with a Twist
Also do balloon creations
Location: 350 Plain St.
      Bridgewater, MA 02324
Ph: 508-697-2306
      508-868-1572 (daytime)
Web: www.funfaceswithatwist.com
Email: funfaceswithatwist@yahoo.com
Contact: Dick & Sue Moberg

Happy Face Painting & Party Art
Location: Worcester, MA
Ph: 508-769-1620
Web: www.happyfacepainting.com
Email: happyfacepainting@yahoo.com
Contact: Roberta Mandella

The Painted Face! Party Art
Location: Mendon, MA 01756
Ph: 508-864-8125
Web: www.maryannfacepainting.com
Email: mycolehenry@hotmail.com

Henna Artists

Deepal Vora
Location: Boston, MA
Ph: 781-281-0632
              781-526-6042
Web: http://hennabydeepal.tripod.com
Email: hennabydeepal@yahoo.com

Magicians, Jugglers & Ventriloquists

Awesome Robb
Location: Whitman, MA 02382
Ph: 781-523-1147
Web: www.awesomerobb.com
Email: magic@awesomerobb.com
Contact: Robb Preskins

Bonaparte
Location: 52A West Eagle St.
Boston, MA 02128
Ph: 617-561-9152
Web: www.bonapartemagic.com
Email: info@bonapartemagic.com

Franc Karpo
Location: Framingham, MA
Ph: 978-274-5613
Web: www.amazingkidsmagic.com
Email: franc@amazingkidsmagic.com

Jenny the Juggler Entertainment
Mailing Address:
280 Brookline St. Suite 2R
Cambridge, MA 02139
Ph: 617-562-5758
Web: www.jennythejuggler.com
Email: jenny@jennythejuggler.com

Magic & Balloons by George
Location: Leicester, MA 01524
Ph: 508-892-4391
Email: magic.balloons@verizon.net

The Magic of David Hall
Location: Boston MA
Ph: 857-205-1883
Web: www.magicofdavidhall.com
Email: magicofdavidhall@mac.com

Mr Magichead
Location: PO Box 1201
  Worcester, MA 01605
Ph: 508-753-2266
Web: www.mrmagichead.com
Email: john@mrmagichead.com
Contact: John Sullivan

Professor Dan The Magic Man
Location: Melrose, MA
Ph: 617-851-0218
Web: www.bostonmagicman.com
Email: dannyhustle@gmail.com

Steve Charette
See also Entertainment Vendors: Disc Jockeys
Location: Worcester, MA 01605
Ph: 508-210-0340
  508-926-9955
Web: www.magicsteve.com
Email: presto13@hotmail.com

Steve Zany

Location:	Attleboro, MA 02703
Ph:	800-828-4662
Web:	www.zanymagic.com
Email:	stevezany@zanymagic.com

Tim "The Magician" David

Location:	Taunton, MA 02780
Ph:	(508) 494-8872
Web:	www.timthemagician.com
Email:	tim@timthemagician.com

Tommy James, Magician

Location:	11 Sharon Ave
	Norfolk, MA 02056
Ph:	508-384-2625
Web:	www.tommyjamesmagic.com
Email:	tommyjamesmagic@yahoo.com

Musicians

Cheryl Melody/Cheryl Melody Productions
Location: PO Box 251
Hopkinton, MA 01748
Ph: 508-435-6198
Web: www.cherymelody.com
www.cherylmelodymusic.com
Email: chermelody@aol.com

jeanniemack
Location: 73 Water St.
Danvers, MA 01923
Ph: 978-762-9747
Web: www.jeanniemack.com
Email: jeanniemack87@yahoo.com

Jon Nelson
Location: Rhode Island
Ph: 617-461-4559
Web: www.jonsongs.com
Email: jonnelsonmusic@gmail.com

Mike "The Music Man" Slattery
Location: Bolton, MA 01740
Ph: 978-779-6789
Web: www.mikethemusicman.com
Email: mcslatts@yahoo.com

Music with Philip

Location:	77 Walker Rd
	Swampscott MA 01907
Ph:	617-818-0346
Web:	www.musicwithphilip.com
Email:	songphil@rcn.com
Contact:	Philip Alexander

Rhythm Kids African Drumming

Location:	PO Box 8
	Concord MA 01742
Ph:	888-569-0712
Web:	www.rhythmkids.com
Email:	rhythmkids@gmail.com

Puppet Shows

Gerwick Puppets
Location: 6 Wood Street
                Southboro, MA 01772
Ph: 508-481-6837
Web: www.gerwickpuppets.com
Email: deborahcostine@verizon.net

Magpie Puppets
Location: Medford, MA
Ph: 781-391-6450
Web: www.magpiepuppets.com
Email: magpie1976@juno.com

Pumpernickel Puppets
Location: 61 Park Ave
                Worcester, MA 01605
Ph: 508-799-4814
Web: www.pumpernickelpuppets.com
Email: puppets2go@aol.com

Rosalita's Puppets
Location: Waltham, MA
Ph: 617-633-2832
Web: www.rosalitaspuppets.com
Email: pheodes@aol.com
Contact: Charlotte Ann Dore

You & Me Puppets
Location: 74 Hillcrest Road
                Reading, MA 01867
Ph: 781-944-0965
Web: www.youandmepuppets.com
Email: jaohare@gmail.com
Contact: Judith O'Hare

Science & Cooking

Let's Play Chef
Location: Hingham, MA 02043
Mailing Address:
    PO Box 709
    Hingham, MA 02043
Ph: 781-987-4836
Web: www.lets-play-chef.com
Email: Katie@lets-play-chef.com

Mad Science of Greater Boston
Location: 37 Whitcomb Street
    Waltham MA 02453
Ph: 781-899-6006
Web: www.madscience.org/greaterboston
Email: msboston@flash.net
Contact: Lynne Larkin

Mad Science of Southern MA & RI
Location: 77 Weaver St.
    Fall River, MA 02720
Ph: 800-748-7134
Web: www.madscience.org/southernmass
Email: mail@madsciencesmari.com

The Magic of Science

Location:	109 Colby Rd
	Weare, NH 03281
Ph:	508-273-6477
Web:	www.themagicofscience.com
Email:	magicofscience@comcast.net
Contact:	Michael Koski

Sabine's Cuisine

Location:	Hopkinton, MA 01748
Ph:	774-292-6766
Web:	http://sabinescuisine.net/
Email:	sabine@sabinescuisine.net

Sports & Dance

Altitude Rocks

Location:	Boston, MA
Ph:	800-862-5462
Web:	www.altituderocks.com
Email:	info@altituderocks.com

Barefoot Arts

Location:	10 Hartshorne Rd
	Wakefield, MA 01880
Ph:	617-549-9228
Web:	www.barefootarts.org
Email:	susan@barefootarts.org

Kinderdance

Location:	Auburn, MA 01501
Ph:	508-864-0022
Web:	www.kinderdance.com
Email:	kinderdancekids@charter.net

Knucklebones: for the love of play!

Location:	PO Box 381589
	Cambridge MA 02338
Ph:	617-851-2928
Fax:	617-449-9609
Web:	www.knucklebones.us
Email:	info@knucklebones.us

Let's Love Music, Musical Adventure Birthday

Location:	Kingston, MA 02364
Ph:	781-582-2534
Web:	www.letslovemusic.com
Email:	info@letslovemusic.com

Tumble Bus: A Gym on Wheels

Location:	Northboro, MA 01532
Ph:	508-393-5287
Web:	www.tumblebus-mass.com
Email:	info@tumblebus-mass.com

Storytellers & Costumed Characters

Characters
Location: PO Box 546
                Milton MA 02186
Ph: 617-296-0206
Web: http://characters4fun.blogspot.com
Email: characters4kids@aol.com

Copacabana Entertainment
Mailing Address:
                PO Box 60528
                Worcester, MA 01606
Ph: 508-853-4257
Web: www.copacabanaent.com
Email: princess@copacabanaent.com

Ed the Wizard
Location: 192 West Main St.
                Orange, MA 01364
Ph: 978-544-8092
Web: www.edthewizard.com
Email: edthewizard@edthewizard.com

Jungle Jim
Location: Cambridge, MA
Ph: 617-223-1700
Web: www.junglejimboston.com
Email: email@junglejimboston.com

Marianne Donnelly

Location: Jamaica Plain, MA 02130
Ph: 617-983-1183
Web: www.coraconnection.com/md

Mister J's Birthday Plays

Location: Roslindale MA 02131
Ph: 617-327-1992
Web: www.users.rcn.com/misterj
Email: misterj@rcn.com

Mother-N-Goose

Location: Worcester, MA 01610
Ph: 774-242-7034
Web: www.mother-n-goose.com
Email: info@motherngoose.com

Unique Entertainment

A Fire Truck for All Occasions
Location: Pembroke, MA 02359
Ph: 781-293-2900
Web: www.afiretruckforall.com

Grade A Hypnosis
Location: 86A Vernon St.
    Worcester, MA 01610
Ph: 508-688-0946
Web: www.gradeahypnosis.com
Email: contact@gradeahypnosis.com

Hurdy Gurdy Monkey & Me LLC
Location: PO Box 600273
    Newton MA 02460
Ph/Vm: 617-964-3074
Fax: 617-964-3275
Web: www.hurdgygurdymonkeyandme.com
Email: hurdygurdy4fun@gmail.com

Ultimate Treasure Hunts
Mailing Address:
          PO Box 974
          Exeter, NH 03833
Ph: 603-772-8772 (office)
          603-978-2815 (cell)
Web: www.ultimatetreasurehunts.com
Email: info@ultimatetreasurehunts.com

Watch Me Grow Productions: Music Video Parties
See also Product Vendors: Videographers
Location: Holden, MA 01520
Ph: 508-852-3749
Web: www.watchmegrowproductions.com
Email: amy@watchmegrowproductions.com

Birthday Locations

Amusement & Creative Play

CoCo Key Water Resort
Web: www.cocokeywaterresort.com
Locations: 50 Ferncroft Road
              Danvers MA 01923
              Ph: 978-777-2500
              Email: rperez@sheratonferncroft.com

              150 Royal Plaza Drive
              Fitchburg, MA 01420
              Ph: 978-343-4006
              Email: lisa.weissman@rplaza.com

Game Universe
Location: 1251 Worcester Rd.
              Framingham, MA 01701
Ph: 508 370-4263
Web: www.myspace.com/gameuniverse

Gymboree Play & Music
Web: www.gymboreeclasses.com
Locations: Intrsctn. Rt. 2A & Nagog Park
              Acton, MA 01720
              Ph: 978-263-9828
              Email:
              actonma@gymboreeclasses.com

              Shawsheen Village Commerce Center
              16 Haverhill St 3rd floor
              (Rt. 133) Andover, MA 01810
              Ph: 781-229-1886
              Email: abgymboree@comcast.net

Gymboree Play & Music, continued

Corporate Place
99 South Bedford St #6
Burlington, MA 01803
Ph: 781-229-1886
Email: abgymboree@comcast.net

109 Oak St.
Newton, MA
Ph: 617-244-2988
Email:
newtonma@gymboreeclasses.com

293 Washington St (Rt. 53)
Norwell, MA 02061
Email:
norwellma@gymboreeclasses.com

101 Falls Blvd
Quincy, MA 02169
Ph: 617-479-5444
Email:
quincyma@gymboreeclasses.com

Jillian's Boston
See also Bowling: Lucky Strike
Location: 145 Ipswich St.
                       Boston, MA 02215
Ph: 617-437-0300
Web: www.jilliansboston.com
Email: functions@jilliansboston.com

Jillian's Worcester
Location: 315 Grove St.
                 Worcester, MA 01605
Ph: 508-793-0900
Web: www.jilliansbilliards.com

Kids Club Funland
Location: 500 Providence Turnpike
                 Norwood, MA 02062
Ph: 781-762-7007
Web: www.kidsclubfunland.com

Kids Funstop
Location: 1580 VFW Parkway
                 West Roxbury, MA 02132
Ph: 617-325-0800
Web: www.kidsfunstop.com
Email: info@kidsfunstop.com

Perpetual Motion Indoor Playground
Location: 345 Chelmsford St.
                 Lowell, MA 01851
Ph: 978-452-0777
Web: http://perpetualmotioninc.com
Email: perpetualmotion@conversent.net

Beauty and Princess Parties

A Girl's Place
Location:	100 Cummings Center Suite 131Q
	Beverly, MA 01915
Ph:	978-922-2799
Web:	www.a-girls-place.com
Email:	a-girls-place@comcast.net

Girl Talk at the Spa
Location:	1149 Walnut Street
	Newton Highlands, MA 02461
Ph:	617-796-9700
Web:	www.girltalkatthespa.com
Email:	bravech@verizon.net

Art Studios & Museums

Artbeat LLC, the Creativity Store
Web: www.artbeatonline.com
Locations: 9 Summer St
                Franklin, MA 02038
                Ph: 508-528-5001
                Email: franklin@artbeatonline.com
                Contact: Jan Whitted

                212A Massachusetts Ave
                Arlington, MA
                Ph: 781-646-2200
                Email: Arlington@artbeatonline.com

Art on the Spot
Location: 337 West Grove St.
               Middleboro, MA 02346
Ph: 508-947-2278
Web: www.artonthespot.com
Email: artonthespot@hotmail.com

Artworks
Location: 263 North Main St.
               Mansfield, MA 02048
Ph: 508-339-0855
Web: www.kristijohnstonartworks.com
Email: Kristin@kristijohnstonartworks.com

Brookline Arts Center
Location: 86 Monmouth St.
               Brookline, MA 02446
Ph: 617-566-5715
Web: www.brooklineartscenter.com
Email: bac@brooklineartscenter.com

(The) Clayground

Location: 65 James St.
       Worcester, MA 01603
Ph: 508-755-7776
Web: www.theclaygroundma.com
Email: theclaygroundworcester@gmail.com

Create & Celebrate

Location: Essex Plaza: 471 Essex St.
       Saugus, MA 01906
Ph: 781-233-7997
Web: www.createandcelebrate.net
Email: juddou@comcast.net

Danforth Museum of Art

Location: 123 Union Ave
       Framingham, MA 01702
Ph: 508-620-0050 x16
Web: www.danforthmuseum.org
Email: jharris@danforthmuseum.org
Contact: Jenn Harris, Assistant Director
       of Development & Marketing

Feat of Clay

Location: 454 Washington St.
       Norwell, MA 02061
Ph: 781-659-2250
Web: www.featofclaypottery.com
Email: admin@featofclaypottery.com

Hands on 4 Kidz

Location: 50 Main St
Gardner, MA 01440
Ph: 978-632-2815
Web: www.handson4kidz.com
Email: handson4kidz@aol.com

It's 2 Dye 4

Location: 312 Tosea Dr.
Stoughton MA 02072
Ph: 781-344-3937
Web: http://its2dye4.com/
Email: alyssa@its2dye4.com
Contact: Alyssa

Not Simply Beads

Location: Village Landing Marketplace
170 Water St.
Plymouth, MA 02360
Ph: 508-747-9222
Web: www.notsimplybeads.com
Email: Nicole@notsimplybeads.com

Party Paints N' Pottery

Location: 58 East Central St.
Franklin, MA 02038
Ph: 508-520-3221
Web: www.paintsandpottery.com
Email: info@paintsandpottery.com

Plaster Fun Time

Web: www.plasterfuntime.com
Email: joe@plasterfuntime.com
Locations: 121 Pearl St
              Braintree, MA 02184
              Ph: 781-849-8400

              113 Drum Hill Rd
              Chelmsford, MA 01824
              Ph: 978-452-2700

              691 Providence Highway
              Dedham, MA 02026
              Ph: 781-326-4445

              209 North Main St.
              Natick, MA 01760
              Ph: 508-651-7673

              118 Needham St.
              Newton Upper Falls, MA 02464
              Ph: 617-244-6080

              347 Man St.
              Reading, MA 01867
              Ph: 781-944-6383

              400 Highland Ave
              Salem, MA 01970
              Ph: 978-745-7788

Pottery Isle

Location: The Tannery
                50 Water St. Suite 138
                Newburyport, MA 01950
Ph: 978-499-3999
Web: www.potteryisle.com
Email: Kathleen@potteryisle.com

Bowling Alleys

Bogey Lanes

Location: 199 North Brookfield Rd
East Brookfield, MA 01515

Mailing Address:
PO Box 439
East Brookfield, MA 01515

Ph: 508-867-6629
Web: www.bogeylanes.com
Email: info@bogeylanes.com

Boston Bowl

Location: 820 Morrissey Blvd.
Boston, MA

Ph: 617-825-3800
Web: www.bostonbowl.com
Email: john@bostonbowl.com

Colonial Bowling Center

Location: 1055 South Main St.
South Weymouth, MA 02190

Ph: 781-335-2906

Ficco's Bowladrome

Location:	300 East Central St.
	Franklin, MA 02038
Ph:	508-528-1142
Fax:	508-528-2828
Web:	www.ficcosbowl.com
Email:	timothy.ficco@verizon.net

Lanes & Games

Location:	195 Concord Turnpike
	(Rt. 2 East)
	Cambridge, MA 02140
Ph:	617-876-5533
Web:	www.lanesandgames.com
Email:	lanesandgames@verizon.net

Lucky Strike

See Amusement & Creative Play: Jillian's Boston

Location:	145 Ipswich St.
	Boston, MA 02215
Ph:	617-437-0300
Web:	www.luckystrikeboston.com
Email:	functions@jilliansboston.com

Needham Bowlaway

Location:	16 Chestnut St.
	Needham, MA 02492
Ph:	781-444-9614
Web:	www.needhambowlaway.com
Email:	info@needhambowlaway.com

North Bowl Lanes
Location: 71 East Washington St.
                N. Attleboro, MA 02760
Ph: 508-695-9333
Web: www.northbowllanes.com
Email: info@northbowllanes.com

Pinz Entertainment
Location: 110 South Main Street
                Milford MA 01757
Ph: 508-473-6611
Web: www.pinzbowl.com
Email: david@pinzbowl.com
Contact: David Breen

Stoughton Sports Center
*soon to be Tiki Bowl
(same location-listed in the indexes as both)
Location: 590 Washington St.
                Stoughton, MA
Ph: 781-344-3321
Web: www.stoughtonsportscenter.com
Email: info@stoughtonsportscenter.com

Dance Centers & Studios

Dance It Up Dance Center
Location: 36 North Main St.
              North Grafton, MA 01536
Ph: 508-839-1648
Fax: 508-839-5946
Web: www.danceitup.com
Email: danceandplay@gmail.com

Diva Dance Parties
Location: 53 Main St.
              Kingston, MA 02364
Ph: 781-585-0330
Web: www.divadanceparties.com
Email: divadance@verizon.net

Joanne Langione Dance Center
Location: 35 Border St.
              West Newton, MA 02465
Ph: 617-969-8724
Web: www.jldancecenter.com
Email: info@jldancecenter.com

In Sync Dance Company
Locations: 5 Thacher St.
              Milton, MA 02186

              300 Bridge St.
              Weymouth, MA 02191
Ph: 617-696-9331 (both locations)
Web: www.insyncdance.com
Email: insyncdance@comcast.net

Gymnastics

Exxcel Gymnastics & Climbing
Location: 88 Wells Ave
                Newton, MA 02459
Ph: 617-244-3300
Web: www.exxcel.net
Email: office@exxcel.net

Gym Kids Gymnastics
Location: Main Street Mercantile Plaza
                North Eastham, MA 02651
Mailing Address:
                PO Box 954
                North Eastham, MA 02651
Ph: 508-240-5747
Web: www.capegymkids.com
Email: info@capegymkids.com

Gym Hutt Gymnastics
Location: 84 Pierce Ave
                Lakeville MA 02347
Ph: 508-823-2299
Web: www.gymhutt.com
Email: angela9598@aol.com

Kaleidescope Gymnastics
Location: 378 Marion Rd
                Wareham, MA 02571
Ph: 508-291-1870
Web: www.kodg.com
Email: kodg@comcast.net

Meridien Gymnastics & Youth Fitness

Location: 871 West Broadway
               Gardner MA 01440
Ph: 978-630-1100
Email: meridian.gymnastics@verizon.net

Nashoba Gymnastics Academy

Location: 49 Powers Rd
               Westford, MA 01886
Ph: 978-692-9907
Fax: 978-589-9798
Web: www.onestopfun.com
Email: onestopfun@charter.net
Contact: Glen Mair

Planet Gymnastics

Location: 7 Strathmore Rd.
               Natick, MA 01760
Ph: 508-647-1777
Web: www.planetgym.com
Email: info@planetgym.com

Gyms & Activity Centers

Jump on In

Location: 100 Phoenix Ave
              Lowell, MA 01852
Ph: 978-453-9700
Web: www.jumponinfun.com
Email: info@jumponinfun.com

Little Gym

Web: www.thelittlegym.com
Locations:
Also Pembroke, Raynham,
Westboro, & West Roxbury

29 Andover St. (Rt. 114)
Danvers, MA 01923
Ph: 978-777-7977
Web: www.tlgdanversma.com
Email:
tlgdanversma@thelittlegym.com

222 Great Rd. Suite 1
Littleton, MA 01460
Ph: 978-952-6600
Web: www.tlglittletonma.com
Email:
tlglittletonma@thelittlegym.com

74 Main St. Medway, MA 02053
Ph: 508-533-9405
Web: www.tlgmedway.com
Email:
tlgmedwayma@thelittlegym.com

Little Gym, continued

260 West Cummings Park
Woburn, MA 01801
Ph: 781-933-3388
Web: www.tlgwoburnma.com
Email:
tlgwoburnma@thelittlegym.com

Monkey Joe's

Location: 10 Newbury St.
Danvers, MA 01923
Ph: 978-739-8099
Web: www.monkeyjoes.com
Email: axelcolle@monkeyjoes.com

Munchkin Land

Location: 30 Oak St.
Westboro, MA 01581
Ph: 508-366-7799
Web: www.munchkin-land.org
Email: giguere6@live.com

My Gym

Web: www.mygymboston.com
(Boston, Newton & Walpole)
www.mygym.com
(National Website)

Locations:
Also Kingston & Norwell
1065 Commonwealth Ave
Boston, MA 02215
Ph: 617-789-3669
Email:
bostonstaff@mygymboston.com

My Gym, continued

855 Worcester Rd
(Rt. 9 West)
Framingham, MA 01701
Ph: 508-370-9496
Email:
mygymframingham@yahoo.com

188 Needham St.
Newton, MA 02464
Ph: 617-243-9496
Email:
newtonstaff@mygymboston.com

677 Main St.
Walpole, MA 02081
Ph: 508-850-9992
Email:
walpolestaff@mygymboston.com

362 Cambridge Rd.
Woburn, MA 01801
Ph: 781-376-9102
Email: ourkidsgym@aol.com

Together in Motion
Location: 1 Broadway
                 Arlington, MA 02474
Ph: 781-643-1377
Web: www.togetherinmotion.com
Email: info@togetherinmotion.com

Ice Skating Rinks

Bay State Blades
24 ice skating rinks in Massachusetts
*out of book coverage area

Web: www.baystateblades.com
Email: info@baystateblades.com
Contact: Danielle Affsa
Locations: Horgan Skating Rink
           400 Oxford St.
           N. Auburn, MA
           Ph: 508-832-7201

           Asiaf Skating Rink
           Forest Avenue Extension
           Brockton, MA
           Ph: 508-583-6804

           Ice Palace
           36 Ray Ave
           Burlington, MA 01803
           Ph: 781-272-9517

           Simoni Arena
           155 Gore St.
           Cambridge, MA
           Ph: 617-354-9523

           Porrazzo Skating Rink
           Constitution Beach
           East Boston, MA
           Ph: 617-567-9571

           Allied Veteran's Skating Rink
           65 Elm St.
           Everett, MA
           Ph: 617-389-3684

Arthur R. Driscoll Memorial
Skating Rink
272 Elsbre St.
Fall River, MA
Ph: 508-679-3274

Wallace Civic Center
100 John Fitch Highway
Fitchburg, MA
Ph: 978-345-7593

Staff Sgt. Robert Pirelli
Veterans Memorial Skating Rink
Panther Way
Franklin, MA
Ph: 508-541-7024

Veteran's Skating Rink
45 Veteran's Dr.
Gardner, MA
Ph: 978-632-4310

*Collins-Moylan
Memorial Skating Rink 5
Barr Ave
Greenfield, MA
Ph: 413-772-6891

*Henry J. Fitzpatrick Skating Rink
575 Maple St.
Holyoke, MA
Ph: 413-532-2929

Connery Memorial Skating Rink
182 Shepard St.
Lynn, MA
Ph: 781-599-9474

John J. Navin Skating Rink
451 Bolton St
Marlboro, MA
Ph: 508-624-5580

William L. Chase Arena
35 Windsor Ave
Natick, MA
Ph:508-655-1013

Stephen Hetland
Memorial Skating Rink
350 Hathaway Blvd.
New Bedford, MA
Ph: 508-999-9051

Chelmsford Forum
2 Brick Kiln Rd
North Billerica, MA
Ph: 978-670-3700

John A. Armstrong
Memorial Skating Rink
Long Pond Rd.
Plymouth, MA
Ph: 508-746-8825

Cronin Memorial Skating Rink
850 Revere Beach Pkwy
Revere, MA
Ph: 781-284-9491

Cyr Skating Rink
200 Trafton Rd.
Springfield, MA
Ph: 413-787-6438

Ray Smead Memorial Skating Rink
1780 Roosevelt Ave
Springfield, MA
Ph: 413-781-2599

Theodore Aleixo Skating Rink
Gordon Owen Riverway
Taunton, MA
Ph: 508-824-4987

Jim Roche Community Arena
1275 VFW Pkwy
West Roxbury, MA
Ph: 617-323-9512

Charles J. Buffone Skating Rink
284 Lake Ave
Worcester, MA
Ph: 508-799-0910

Interactive & Educational Fun Venues

Leventhal-Sidman Jewish Community Center
Location: 333 Nahanton St.
                Newton, MA 02459
Ph: 617-558-6419
Web: www.lsjcc.org/home/birthday.html
Email: mwyman@jccgb.org

Noodle Noggin N' Bean Inc
Location: 38 SW Cutoff (Rt. 20)
                Northboro MA 01532
Ph: 508-351-7060
Fax: 508 351-7061
Web: www.noodlenogginnbean.com
Email: nnnb@noodlenogginnbean.com
Contact: Linda H. Stockhaus, President

Thornton Burgess Society
At the Green Briar Nature Center
Location: 6 Discovery Hill Rd
                East Sandwich, MA
Ph: 508-888-6870 x13
Web: www.thorntonburgess.org
Email: mary.beers@thorntonburgess.org

Lazer Tag

LaserCraze

Location:	1600 Osgood St.
	North Andover, MA
Ph:	978-689-7700
Web:	www.lasercraze.us
Email:	play@lasercraze.us

Lazer Gate

Location:	288 Plymouth Ave
	Fall River, MA 02721
Ph:	508-730-1230
Web:	www.lazergate.com
Email:	information@lazergate.com

Miniature Golf

Bass River Sports World
Skull Island Adventure Golf
See also Birthday Locations: Sports Venues
Location: 934 Route 28
                  South Yarmouth, MA 02664
Ph: 508-398-6070 (business)
                  774-212-4533
                  (birthdays, corporate/group bookings)
Web: www.bassriversportsworld.com
Email: brswsi@aol.com

Monster Mini Golf
Indoors
Web: www.monsterminigolf.com
Locations:
Also Fairhaven, Seekonk & Webster

                  10 Newbury St.
                  Danvers, MA 01923
                  Ph: 978-762-4800
                  Email: minigolfconcepts@verizon.net
                  Contact: Peter Cali

                  1560 Boston Providence Highway
                  Norwood, MA 02062
                  Ph: 781-762-3100
                  Email: minigolf@verizon.net
                  Contact: Veronica Swan

Mulligan's Mini Golf

Location: 124 Leominster Rd.

Route 12

Sterling, MA

Mailing Address:

PO Box 426

Sterling, MA 01564

Ph: 978-422-5022

Web: www.mulligansminigolf.com

Email: mulligansminigolf@hotmail.com

Trombetta's Farm

Indoors

Location: 655 Farm Rd.

Marlboro, MA 01752

Ph: 508-485-6429

Web: www.trombettasfarm.com

Email: trombettasfarm@hotmail.com

Museums & Historical Locations

American Textile History Museum
Location: 491 Dutton St.
                  Lowell, MA 01854
Ph: 978-441-0400
Fax: 978-441-1412
Web: www.athm.org
Email: khirbour@athm.org

Battleship Cove & The Fall River Carousel
Location: 5 Water St.
                  Fall River, MA 02722
Mailing Address:
                  PO Box 111
                  Fall River, MA 02722
Ph: 508-678-1100
                  800-533-3194
                  (Toll Free in New England)
Web: www.battleshipcove.org
Email: battleship@battleshipcove.org

Boston Children's Museum
Location: 300 Congress St.
                  Boston, MA 02210
Ph: 617-426-6500 x380
Web: www.bostonchildrensmuseum.org
Email: Andrade@bostonchildrensmuseum.org
Contact: Amanda Andrade,
                  Birthday Party Senior Coordinator

Children's Museum in Easton
Location: 9 Sullivan Ave
                  North Easton, MA 02356
Ph: 508-230-3789
Web: www.childrensmuseumineaston.org
Email: info@childrensmuseumineaston.org

New Bedford Whaling Museum

Location: 18 Johnny Cake Hill Road
New Bedford, MA 02740
Ph: 508-997-0046
Web: www.whalingmuseum.org
Email: specialevents@whalingmuseum.org

Top Fun Aviation Toy Museum

Location: 21 Prichard St.
Fitchburg, MA 01420
(No mail please)
Mailing Address:
PO Box 700
Dracut, MA 01826
Ph: 978-342-2809
Web: www.topfunaviation.com
Email: topfun@attglobal.net

Old Sturbridge Village

Location: 1 Old Sturbridge Village Rd.
Sturbridge, MA 01566
Ph: 508-347-0285
Web: www.osv.org
Email: osved@osv.org

Music Studios

Backyard Jams
Location: 25 Esten Ave
               Pawtucket, RI 02860
Ph: 401-648-7144
Web: www.backyardjams.com
Email: info@backyardjams.com

Limelight Stage & Studios, Inc
Location: 204 Tremont St.
               Boston, MA 02116
Ph: 617-423-0785
Web: www.limelightboston.com
Email: info@limelightboston.com

Mockingbird Studios
Location: 905 South Main St.
               Mansfield, MA
Ph: 508-339-6755
Web: www.mockingbirdstudio.com
Email: markd@mockingbirdweb.com

Paintball Fields

Cape Cod Paintball
Location: Bourne Rotary
                Bourne, MA
Mailing Address:
                PO Box 2358
                East Falmouth, MA 02536
Ph: 508-400-6807
Web: www.capecodpaintball.com
Email: info@capecodpaintball.com

Fox 4 Paintball
Location: 159 Milford St.
                Upton, MA 01568
Ph: 508-529-3694
Fax: 508-529-3699
Web: www.fox4paintball.com
Email: fox4paintball@yahoo.com

Friendly Fire Paintball
Location: 108 Grove St.
                Upton, MA 01568
Ph: 508-529-7400
Fax: 508-529-3274
Web: http://friendlyfirepaintball.com
Email: Linda@friendlyfire-paintball.com

Westend Paintball
Location: 1759 Main St.
                Leicester, MA 01524
Ph: 508-721-0003
Fax: 508-721-0010
Web: www.westendpaintball.com
Email: xfirepaintball@firepaintball.com

Puppet Theaters

Drawbridge Puppets
Location: 1335 Massachusetts Avenue
              Lunenburg, MA 01462
Ph: 800-401-3694
Web: www.drawbridgepuppets.com
Email: drawbridgepuppets@gmail.com
Contact: Paul L'Ecuyer

Puppet Showplace Theatre
Location: 32 Station St
              Brookline MA 02445
Ph: 617-731-6400
Web: www.puppetshowplace.org
Email: info@puppetshowplace.org

Roller Skating Rinks

Carousel Family Fun Center
Web: www.carouselskate.com
Locations: 4 David Drown Blvd
              Fairhaven, MA 02719
              Ph: 508-996-4828
              Email: Fairhaven@carouselskate.com

              1055 Auburn St.
              Whitman, MA 02382
              Ph: 781-857-1286
              Email: Whitman@carouselskate.com

Rollerworld
Location: 425r Broadway
             Saugus MA 01906
Ph: 781-231-1111
Web: www.roller-world.com
Email: mbreen2673@aol.com

Roll on America Family Fun Center
Location: 90 Duval Rd
             Lancaster MA 01523
Ph: 978-537-4010
Web: www.rollonamerica.com
Email: susan@rollonamerican.com
Contact: Susan Perkins

Skateland

Location: 19 Railroad Ave
                Bradford, MA 01835
Mailing Address:
                PO Box 5270
                Bradford, MA 01835
Ph: 978-372-3050
Web: www.skateland.com
Email: info@skateland.org

Science & Nature Locations

Ecotarium
See also Birthday Locations:
Zoos & Other Animal Locations
Location: 222 Harrington Way
                Worcester, MA 01604
Ph: 508-929-2700 &
                508-929-2703 (birthday reservations)
Web: www.ecotarium.org
Email: info@ecotarium.org

Green Meadows Farm
Location: 656 Asbury St.
                South Hamilton, MA 01982
Ph: 978-468-3720
Web: www.gmfarm.com
Email: organicfarmer@comcast.net

Smolak Farms
Location: 315 South Bradford St.
                North Andover, MA 01845
Ph: 978-687-4029
Web: www.smolakfarms.com
Email: smolakfarmstours@aol.com

Stonybrook Wildlife Sanctuary
Location: 108 North St.
                Norfolk, MA 02056
Ph: 508-528-3140
Web: www.massaudobon.org
Email: stonybrook@massaudobon.org

Sports Venues

American Kempo
Web: www.akka.com
Email: akka-staff@akka.com
Locations: 383 Columbia Rd.
           Hanover, MA 02339
           Ph: 781-829-1008

           6 Main St.
           Hanson, MA 02341
           Ph: 781-294-4240

           12 West Water St.
           Rockland, MA 02370
           Ph: 781-878-4011

           170 Middle St.
           Weymouth, MA 02189
           Ph: 781-331-8008

Amesbury Sports Park & New England Soccer School
Location: 12 South Hunt Road
           Amesbury MA 01913
Ph: 978-388-5788 X102
Fax: 978-388-4397
Web: www.amesburysportspark.net
Email: mfranceschi@goslide.com
Contact: Martha Franceschi

Bass River Sports World & Skull Island Adventure Golf

See also Birthday Locations: Miniature Golf

Location:	934 Route 28
	South Yarmouth, MA 02664
Ph:	508-398-6070 (business)
	774-212-4533 (event bookings)
Web:	www.bassriversportsworld.com
Email:	brswsi@aol.com

Boston Trapeze School

Location:	50 Walker's Brook Dr.
	Reading, MA 01867
Ph:	781-942-7800
Web:	http://boston.trapezeschool.com
Email:	boston@trapezeschool.com

Extra Innings

* Outside the book coverage area

Web:	www.extrainnings.us
Locations:	*45 Tennis Rd
	Agawam, MA 01001
	Ph: 413-789-9200
	Email:
	info@extrainnings-agawam.com

38 Southbridge St.
Auburn, MA 01501
Ph: 508-459-2269
Email:
info@extrainnings-auburn.com

Extra Innings, continued

264 South Main St.
Middleton, MA 01949
Ph: 978-762-0668
Email: info@extra-innings.net

6 Old Elm St.
Salisbury, MA 01952
Ph: 978-499-0063
Email:
info@extrainnings-salisbury.com

890 East St.
Tewksbury, MA 01876
Ph: 978-851-1220
Email:
info@extrainnings-tewksbury.com

100 Parker St.
Watertown, MA 02472
Ph: 617-393-3858
Email:
info@extrainnings-agawam.com

319 Manley St.
West Bridgewater, MA 02379
Ph: 508-580-3113
Email:
info@extrainnings-wbridgewater.com

10 Micro Drive
Woburn, MA 01801
Ph: 781-935-2256
Email:
info@extrainnings-woburn.com

Extra Innings, continued

15 Cushing Dr.
Wrentham, MA 02093
Ph: 508-384-8295
Email:
info@extrainnings-wrentham.com

Fore Kicks Sports Complexes

Web: www.forekicks.com
Email: patteager@forekicks.com
(Birthday Party Program Manager)
Locations: 219 Forest St.
Marlboro, MA 01752
Ph: 508-624-4433

10 Pine St.
Norfolk, MA 02053
Ph: 508-384-4433

Guard Up! Family Sportmanship

Location: 141 Middlesex Turnpike
Burlington, MA 01803
Ph: 781-270-4800
Web: www.guardup.com
Email: guardup@guardup.com

John Smith Sports and the Zig Zag Zone

Location: 70 Summer St
Milford MA 01757
Ph: 800-998-7622
Web: www.johnsmithsoccer.com
Email: jssc1@comcast.net

Jungle Plex
Location: 8 Natalie Way
                Plymouth, MA 02360
Ph: 508-830-1411
Fax: 508-830-1099
Web: www.jungleplex.com
Email: info@jungleplex.com

Lighthouse Fitness Rock Climbing Parties
Location: 10 Cordage Park Circle Suite 243
                Plymouth MA 02360
Ph: 508-746-8770
Web: www.lhfcenters.com
Email: jmclean@lhfcenters.com

Metro Rock
Web: www.metrorock.com
Email: info@metrorock.com
Locations: 69 Norman St.
                Everett, MA 02149
                Ph: 617-387-7625

                40 Parker St.
                Newburyport, MA 01950
                Ph: 978-499-7625

New England Sports Academy
Location: 345 University Ave
                Westwood, MA 02090
Ph: 781-493-6345
Web: www.nesacademy.com
Email: mrubin@nesacademy.com

Thundercat Sports

Location:	120 Paul Revere Rd
	Arlington, MA 02476
Ph:	617-499-4820
Web:	www.thundercatsports.com
Email:	info@thundercatsports.com

Weymouth Club

Location:	75 Finnell Dr.
	Weymouth, MA 02188
Ph:	781-337-4600
Fax:	781-331-9155
Web:	www.weymouthclub.com
Email:	events@weymouthclub.com

Theme Party Locations

Imajine That
Location:	354 Merrimack St., 2nd floor
	Lawrence, MA 01843
Ph:	978-682-5338
Web:	www.imajinethat.com
Email:	parties@imajinethat.com

Pick A Party
Location:	20 East St.
	Hanover, MA 02339
Ph:	781-588-2274
	781-826-1300
Web:	www.pickapartyatbase.com
Email:	pickaparty@comcast.net

Theme Restaurants

Rainforest Café
Location: Burlington Mall
                75 Middlesex Tnpk Space 1051
                Burlington MA 01803
Ph: 781-272-7555
Web: www.rainforestcafe.com

Unique Venues

Arrowhead Acres

Location: 92 Aldrich St.
             Rt. 98
             Uxbridge, MA 01569
Ph: 508-278-5017
             508-847-1220 (Cell)
Fax: 508-278-3841
Web: www.arrowheadacres.com
Email: dave@arrowheadacres.com

YMCA & YWCA

Constitution Inn YMCA
Location: 150 Third Ave
                Charlestown, MA 02129
Ph: 617-241-8400 x3019
Fax: 617-241-2856
Web: www.ymcaboston.org
Email: bchaisson@ymcaboston.org

Dorchester YMCA
Location: 776 Washington St.
                Dorchester, MA 02124
Ph: 617-326-7938
Web: www.ymcaboston.org
Email: dmurray-mccarthy@ymcaboston.org

Merrimack Valley YMCA
Web: www.mvymca.org
Locations: 165 Haverhill St.
                Andover, MA 01810
                Ph: 978-685-3541
                Email: lvalenti@mvymca.org

                40 Lawrence St.
                Lawrence, MA 01840
                Ph: 978-686-6191
                Email: csoohoo@mvymca.org

                129 Haverhill St
                Methuen, MA 01844
                Ph: 978-683-5266
                Email: jlabelle@mvymca.org

North Suburban YMCA of Greater Boston

Location: 137 Lexington St.
                Woburn, MA 01801
Ph: 781-935-3270 x204
Web: www.ymcaboston.org/woburn/
Email: skovalchek@ymcaboston.org

Waltham YMCA

Location: 725 Lexington St.
                Waltham, MA 02452
Ph: 781-894-5295 x105
Web: www.ymcaboston.org/waltham
Email: jweller@ymcaboston.org

YWCA of Central Massachusetts

Location: 1 Salem Square
                Worcester, MA 01608
Ph: 508-767-2505 x3039
Web: www.ywcaworcester.org
Email: gmm@ywcaworcester.org

Yoga Studios

Absolute Yoga:
Kids Yoga Parties with Amy Harper
Location: 77 West Main St. #212
                 Hopkinton, MA 01748
Ph: 508-435-3366
Web: www.absoluteyoga.net
Email: info@absoluteyoga.net

Sweet Pea Yoga
Location: 77 West Main St. #212
                 Hopkinton, MA 01748
Ph: 508-981-3244
Web: www.sweetpeayoga.com
Email: info@sweetpeayoga.com

Zoos & Other Animal Locations

Butterfly Place
Location: 120 Tyngsboro Rd
               Westford, MA 01886
Ph: 978-392-0955
Web: www.butterflyplace-ma.com
Email: bflybut@aol.com

Capron Park Zoo
Location: 201 County Street
               Attleboro MA 02703
Ph: 508-222-6202
Web: www.capronparkzoo.com
Email: cpzstochrer@yahoo.com
Contact: Melanie Stoehrer,
               Curator of Education

Ecotarium
See also Birthday Locations: Science & Nature
Location: 222 Harrington Way
               Worcester, MA 01604
Ph: 508-929-2700
               508-929-2703 (birthday reservations)
Web: www.ecotarium.org
Email: info@ecotarium.org

Southwicks Zoo
Location: 2 Southwick Street
               Mendon MA 01756
Ph: 800-258-9182 X209
Web: www.southwickszoo.com
               www.earthltd.org
Email: Betsey@southwickszoo.com
Contact: Betsey Brewer

Birthday Town Index

Barnstable County

Bristol County

Essex County

Haverhill

Lawrence

Lynn

Melrose

Methuen

Middleton

Newburyport

North Andover

Franklin County

Middlesex County

Cambridge

Charlestown

Chelmsford

Concord

Everett

Framingham

Newton

North Billerica

North Reading

Reading

Somerville

Sudbury

Woburn

Norfolk County

Milton

Needham

Norfolk

Norwood

Quincy

South Weymouth

Stoughton

Plymouth County

Abington

Bridgewater

Brockton

East Bridgewater

Hanover

Hanson

Hingham

Kingston

Lakeville

Middleboro

Norwell

Plymouth

Plympton

Rockland

Wareham

West Bridgewater

West Wareham

Whitman

Suffolk County

Boston

Dorchester

East Boston

Jamaica Plain

Revere

Roslindale

West Roxbury

Winthrop

Worcester County

Holden

Lancaster

Leicester

Lunenburg

Mendon

Milford

Northborough

North Grafton

Worcester

Massachusetts
Outside the Book's Coverage Area

New Hampshire

Rhode Island

Index

www.ingramcontent.com/pod-product-compliance
Lightning Source LLC
Chambersburg PA
CBHW060631290526
45793CB00001B/212